FOREWORD

For Young Writers' latest competition This Is Me, we asked primary school pupils to look inside themselves, to think about what makes them unique, and then write a poem about it! They rose to the challenge magnificently and the result is this fantastic collection of poems in a variety of poetic styles.

Here at Young Writers our aim is to encourage creativity in children and to inspire a love of the written word, so it's great to get such an amazing response, with some absolutely fantastic poems. It's important for children to focus on and celebrate themselves and this competition allowed them to write freely and honestly, celebrating what makes them great, expressing their hopes and fears, or simply writing about their favourite things. This Is Me gave them the power of words. The result is a collection of inspirational and moving poems that also showcase their creativity and writing ability.

I'd like to congratulate all the young poets in this anthology, I hope this inspires them to continue with their creative writing.

CONTENTS

Cawood CE Primary School, Cawood

George Freeman (10)	61
Elizabeth Dean (9)	62
Holly Hindmarch (10)	63
Megan Stephenson (10)	64
Maisy Vinton (9)	65
Daniel Murray (10)	66
Amber Smales (10)	67
Dylan Davenport (9)	68
Madison Jessop	69
Charlie Holdcroft (9)	70
Alfie Brooke (9)	71
Jonah Hood (8)	72
Alana Thorpe (10)	73

Dothill Primary School, Wellington

Finlay Langard-Brown (10)	74
Sophia Haycock (10)	76
Daisy Swales (9)	78
Jamie-Leigh Parsons (10)	79
Kayleigh Holehouse (9)	80
Franklin Carpenter (10)	81
Thomas Olliver (10)	82
Faye Duff (10)	83
Lucie Hayward (9)	84
Bella Wall (8)	85
Harriet Archer-Jones (10)	86

Faraday School, Poplar

Glenn Tong (7)	87
Ishaan Sutaria (7)	88
Ira Kishore (8)	89
Emerson Krasilnick (8)	90
Akshay Siddharth (8)	91
Chidinma Blackwell (8)	92
Alfie Hobbs (8)	93
Benjamin Whatling (7)	94
Oscar Ramsbottom (7)	95
Sienna Lodhia (7)	96

Theia Kothari (7)	97
Isabelle Clancy (7)	98
Jagger Hou (8)	99
Banner Thorne (7)	100
Dixie Pittuck (8)	101
Owen Blanchandin (8)	102
Isabella Chen (7)	103

New Rush Hall School, Ilford

Freddie Williams (11)	104
Tillie Follen (11)	105
Phillip Hurst (10)	106
Marcus Rolston-Jones (11)	107
Sidney Turvey (11)	108

Northcote Primary School, Liverpool

Isabel Walsh (11)	109
Jake Cashen (11)	110
Luke Tillman (11)	111
Raimi Nigel Bature (10)	112
Lacey Matthews (9)	113
Kaitlyn Hamilton-Graney (10)	114
Halle Dwyer (9)	115
Niamh Brown (11)	116
Luca Evason (10)	117
Jennifer Boyd Clarke (11)	118
Archie Willis (11)	119
Lyla Jaycock Fury (10)	120
Adrian Burca (11)	121
Chloe Jones (9)	122
Freddie Baxter (10)	123
Daniel Elliott (11)	124
Aleisha Robinson (11)	125
Macy Parkin (10)	126
Mateo Kulli (11)	127
Daisy Rose McKibbin (10)	128
Poppy-Jo Fairclough (8)	129
Peyton Cliffe (10)	130
Mia O'Brien (10)	131
Jaeden Bloxham (11)	132
Rudy Iurcia (10)	133

THE POWER OF POETRY

Edited By Daisy Job

First published in Great Britain in 2022 by:

Young Writers
Remus House
Coltsfoot Drive
Peterborough
PE2 9BF
Telephone: 01733 890066
Website: www.youngwriters.co.uk

Printed and bound in the UK by BookPrintingUK
Website: www.bookprintinguk.com
YB0516F

Jason Ian Evans (10) 134
Millie Smith-Stoddern (10) 135
Heidi Lindop (11) 136
Estelle Lucia Fernandez (11) 137
Will Henry Cain (11) 138

Our Lady Mother Of The Saviour Catholic Primary School, Palacefields

Jessica Ball (9) 139
Oscar Evans (7) 140
Lily Mayock (9) 141

Parkwood Primary School, Keighley

Imaamah Khan (9) 142
Zakkary Harris (8) 143
Maanya Sathish (7) 144
Konni Bland-Farmery (9) 145

St Brigid's Primary School, Northfield

Mylena Mboungo Guewo (9) 146
Alfie Huggins (10) 148
Ava Djali (8) 149
Hugo Snelgrove-Thompson (9) 150
Isabel Stephen (10) 152
Rachel D (9) 154
Bella Fryer (9) 155
Elyam Teklit (9) 156
Amarise Anyaorah (10) 157
Lukas Tylenis (10) 158
Isabelle Pritchard (8) 159

St Margaret Of Scotland Primary School, South Carbrian

Hayley Muirhead (8) 160
Charlie Smellie (8) 161
Samara-Hope O'Connor (7) 162

St Mary's Catholic Primary School, Newcastle-Under-Lyme

Aqeena Jones (9) 163

St Mary's Catholic Primary School, South Moor

Athulya Edirisingha (9) 164
Mia Purdy (10) 166
Lewis Trelease (10) 167
Rana Ozbek (10) 168
Maddie Corby (9) 170
Gracie McArdle (9) 172
William Leighton (9) 173
Aerys Gray (10) 174
Charleigh Gardner (10) 175
Dylan Gibson (10) 176
Ryan Ingram (9) 177
Mason Proctor (10) 178
Mackenzie Brunskill (10) 179
Mitchell Walton (10) 180
Harry Stanger (10) 181
Charlie Marsden (9) 182

St Mary's CE Academy Walkley, Sheffield

Aris Roussias (8) 183
Ledjon Mustafa (9) 184
Zeenat Ahmadi (9) 185
Jobey Ramjiani (9) 186
Tara Adesola (9) 187
Hazel McMahon (9) 188
Miles Russell (9) 189

Walford Primary School, Walford

Harry England (10) 190
Mario Bundy (11) 191
Arrianne Marangon (11) 192
Maisie Walton (11) 193
Tyler Spiers (9) 194
Isla Matthews (11) 195
Zach Davies (9) 196

| Clemie Goodison | 197 |
| Max Bain (9) | 198 |

Ysgol Hen Felin, Ystrad

Sophie McGuiness (11)	199
Alicia Jones (10)	200
Phoebe Lloyd Szigetvari (11)	201
Jason Jones	202

THE POEMS

This Is Me

This is me

I'm as good as a robot cleaning up, helping my mum

My ears are as fluffy as a rabbit to keep my ears warm

I am as strong as a rhino to protect my family

My teeth are like blades to eat with

I am as warm as a llama, so I'm warm-hearted, not cold

I am as healthy as the dentist to eat yummy snacks

My mouth is as wide as a camel's mouth to eat healthy food

I am as good as the teacher

This is me.

Texas Lee (8)

Beardall Fields Primary And Nursery School, Hucknall

This Is Me

This is me
Feet as fast as a cheetah playing with my friends
Hands like sticks playing with my friends
Legs like a giraffe to fun as fast as I can
Mouth like a hot oven to eat pizza with
Fingers as long as grass to tickle my brother with
This is me.

Ollie Stanley (7)
Beardall Fields Primary And Nursery School, Hucknall

My Life

T rying to help my mom and dad
H uge improvement in the houses which is awesome
I love them very much
S ometimes I'm naughty but I always learn

I love my pets and family
S nowball is my kitten

M e and my brother are happy with our life
E veryone is being kind as usual

M ischievous me is what I used to be
A nd new me is kind and caring
Y arnold is my last name
A ranauskaite is my mom's last name because she's Lithuanian.

Maya Valentina (9)
Bells Farm Primary School, Druids Heath

This Is Me!

I 'm a helpful person with a positive smile,

M um works hard so I like to help out with the washing,

E very day is the best because I ride my bike,

V ery happy when I'm chatting with my family,

E veryone shows respect when we're kind and helpful,

L oving each other every day,

Y ou're all my friends forever,

N ever letting unhappiness take over,

E ven when times are tough.

This is me!

Evelyne Heard (8)

Bells Farm Primary School, Druids Heath

Supersonic

Generous and kind,
Got a super-fast mind!
Maths is the best,
Subtractions, divisions, bring it all on... I never like
to rest!

I jump and I spring,
So I know I'm not a wimp!
I'm a football fan,
I watch all the games as fast as I can!

So this is me,
Sometimes happy and sometimes sad!
I'm supersonic so I try to win.
If I'm feeling sad, well, let's put that thought into
the bin!

Harvey Harper (8)
Bells Farm Primary School, Druids Heath

What Animal Am I?

I am in a scorching hot country yet never hot where I am,
Some have heard of me, some haven't,
I am a mammal and give birth to my children,
I walk on all four feet and make pawprints in the snow,
But I am also a vicious predator, hunting to survive,
I am endangered too so I have to be careful...
What animal am I?

Answer: An Amur leopard (in northern Pakistan).

Maarya Siddiqui (9)
Bells Farm Primary School, Druids Heath

This Is Me

T he generous friend you could have

H as your back whenever you need

I have annoying siblings but that won't stop me from loving them

S ome say I'm rude

I know who I am

S taying with my friends is who I am

M y friends support me whenever I'm feeling down

E xcitement is my goal.

Alexie Langford (9)

Bells Farm Primary School, Druids Heath

This Is Me, Dora!

I'm clever, I'm smart,
I am like Sonic when doing maths,
But worst, I frown in history,
It's mundane, it's boring,

Chinese, English, French,
Super at languages,
Chinese at home,
School is English,

Looking at the rainbow,
Purple has hearts in them,
But brown is very bad,
Also, I love blue and pink.

Dora Huang (8)
Bells Farm Primary School, Druids Heath

The Tiny Little Daisy

T iny in size,
H ave an annoying brother, Alfie,
I love school and gymnastics,
S eeing my family is the best,

I love my mom and dad,
S ometimes I play with my brother,

M y friends are the best to go to when I'm sad,
E verybody is unique.

Daisy Birch (9)
Bells Farm Primary School, Druids Heath

All About Millie The Mildrid

T iny in size,
H ave an annoying sister called Frankie!
I love dogs,
S easide is my favourite place!

I love my cute pets,
S ometimes I make bath bombs!

M e and my 14-year-old cousin play-fight
E lephants are my second favourite animal.

Millie Brown (9)

Bells Farm Primary School, Druids Heath

As Fast As Lightning!

I am a lightning bolt in football boots,
I am a superstar striker,
I am a lover of animals (Hi, Leo my dog!),
I am a lion, strong and brave,
I am as kind as a nurse,
My hair is dark black,
My eyes are black marbles.
This is me!

Jason-Paul Ngambi (8)

Bells Farm Primary School, Druids Heath

What Am I?

You can cuddle me, I'm super soft.
I love to play tug of war with my toy,
I get out of breath easily.
I am very bouncy.
I am extremely playful.
What am I?

Answer: A puppy dog.

Imogen Jones (9)
Bells Farm Primary School, Druids Heath

What Emotion Could I Be?

Going to the beach with the glow of the sun,
Flying high, I'm number 1,
Swimming in the sea, having so much fun,
Lying in the clouds, I feel like I've won!
What emotion am I?

Rawan Zahra (9)
Bells Farm Primary School, Druids Heath

This Is Ziyan!

A kennings poem

I am a...
Animal adorer,
Biscuit dunker,
Book reader,
Craft maker,
Early riser,
Fast runner,
Light sleeper,
And most importantly...
From a-z a happy Ziyan!

Ziyan Zheng (9)
Bells Farm Primary School, Druids Heath

What Am I?

What am I?
We're really slow,
But fast swimmers,
We sleep on trees,
Everything we see
Is a fantastic view!

Answer: A sloth.

George Johnson (9)
Bells Farm Primary School, Druids Heath

What Tree Am I?

I am a bendy tree of all power.
I look beautiful when I flower.
Even when I fall I still keep growing.
But in the winter I start slowing.
In the summer the flowers begin to sprout.
When they came they fight for the best route.
But here comes a day when I start to betray
And I become frayed.
I could be the materials of this jotter.
I am also the name of the tree in Harry Potter,
Just without the weeping.
That is because I am sleeping.
Now it is time to say goodbye.
Also have a guess, what am I?

Answer: A weeping willow.

Ross Griffiths (8)
Broughton-In-Furness CE Primary School, Kepplewray

My Cat

My cat is really leapy
She is also tired and sleepy
When she jumps up on my shoulder it makes me cry
When she sees strangers she is shy
Cassie also is super funny
She jumps so high like a bunny
I look at her, she looks at me
Until birds gather around her tree
Cassie mostly jumps on the table
She messes with a label
When she's outside she's on a log
Until she sees a dog!
She pulls herself tight
Until she's ready to fight
When the fight heals
She plays in fields
She has a purr
I love her.

Evie Earl (7)
Broughton-In-Furness CE Primary School, Kepplewray

An Odd Recipe

You will need:
To love to spend money
Really really funny
Gentle as a bee
A love for sloths.

How to make:
First add in the gentleness then stir in the funny bit!
Now the love to spend money and it will look funny.
The love for sloths comes last as it is the most important bit.
Add a dash of it until it's the colour of a blue tit!
Now you can ice it and decorate it but
Congratulations, you've made me!

Jess Satterthwaite (9)
Broughton-In-Furness CE Primary School, Kepplewray

This Is All About Me

G ymnastics was my hobby a few years ago
Y ellow is a pretty colour
M y favourite animal is a fox
N ever have tomato sauce, I hate tomato sauce
A nd my eyes are as dark as dark chocolate
S ummer is my favourite season
T igers are one of my favourite animals
I love drawing in my room
C limbing is fun
S kateboarding is my hobby.

Delila Livesey (9)

Broughton-In-Furness CE Primary School, Kepplewray

Football Crazy

F ootball is my favourite sport
O n the pitch, I am a super striker
O ff the pitch, I am always eating
T he ball is what I always want
B lue is my favourite colour
A nd I like biking with my family
L oads of people come to watch me play
L ines are where you need to keep the ball in play.

Brook Darwick (9)
Broughton-In-Furness CE Primary School, Kepplewray

All About Me

F arming is what I like

O utside is one of my favourite things to do

O ffside, I'm always offside

T rains are what I like

B all, I like playing football

A eroplanes, I like being on them

L ove is nice

L oud is what I always am.

Jonny Fox (8)

Broughton-In-Furness CE Primary School, Kepplewray

My Favourite Sport

My favourite sport uses a ball
And I love it more than anything,
Anything at all.
It has a net and I'll win a match I bet.
My favourite sport uses a ball
And I love it more than anything,
Anything at all!
What sport is it?

Answer: Tennis.

William Armstrong (8)

Broughton-In-Furness CE Primary School, Kepplewray

What I Am

A rty and called an artist
R elaxed but full of energy
T awny-coloured hair
I nspired by art
S ongwriter, that's what I am
T ennis is my favourite sport
I love animals
C reative and unique, this is me!

Rosie Shufflebottom (9)
Broughton-In-Furness CE Primary School, Kepplewray

All About Me

I'm learning to play football
Like asking people if they're okay
My hair is as curly as my puppy's fur
My eyes are brown like a chocolate bar
Gaming is one of my favourite things to do
I like playing out in the back street
That's all about me.

Finley Burch (9)
Broughton-In-Furness CE Primary School, Kepplewray

Animal Riddle

I'm as slick as a tick,
Faster than a lion.
I'm from Scotland
But don't have an accent.
I fly high up in the sky,
Looking for mice,
They taste very nice.
What am I?

Answer: A golden eagle.

Jack Hull (9)
Broughton-In-Furness CE Primary School, Kepplewray

All About Me

F ood I love
O ranges I like
O utside in the park
T ough like a lion
B uddy is my bird
A long with my friends
L oving family
L ove my sisters.

Rory Lindsay (9)
Broughton-In-Furness CE Primary School, Kepplewray

Me And My Horse

My foal likes to play over and over again,
He tips the water over and over.
He can lick like a dog,
He swims like a fish,
But he is a very cute foal though.

Scarlett Ellwood (9)

Broughton-In-Furness CE Primary School, Kepplewray

All About Me

I like farming,
My favourite animal is a rhino,
My favourite sport is tennis,
I am as strong as a bull,
I love going out on my bike with my friends.

Thomas Lane (10)
Broughton-In-Furness CE Primary School, Kepplewray

What Am I?

I'm an animal too small to see
You don't know anything.
You can see me only from a microscope.
What am I?

Answer: A germ.

Reuben Harris (9)
Broughton-In-Furness CE Primary School, Kepplewray

The Dog De Bordeaux Hunter

This is Hunter.
Hunter is a very kind dog.
I fell over and my sister pretended to punch me
And Hunter protected me
And bumped Willow.

Summer Armstrong (8)
Broughton-In-Furness CE Primary School, Kepplewray

A Normal Day In My Life

I wake up in the morning, make my bed
Brush my teeth and hair
And go to school and play
Then do work, boring!

Ellie Stone (8)
Broughton-In-Furness CE Primary School, Kepplewray

I Am Getting Older

I am a curious boy as cool as the summer breeze,
my million-dollar smile melts people's hearts.
As I am growing older, I am getting bolder.
Soon, I will be tall enough to reach the mountains.
Time is flying by and I'm dreaming of a bright
future whilst I delve deeper finding gold.
My dad says I am a keeper!
I am getting older.

My bubbly personality shines like a glittery
diamond.
I am a floating cloud, always making everyone
proud!
Twinkling sweet melodies on my piano, my voice is
as sweet as silver bells.
On the pitch, I am like a rocket flying into space.
Over time, my passions will change and my
interests will widen,
Whilst I get fond of the new, arguments will fade.
I am getting older.

Gentle like the waves surging onto the shore, the
world is my stage, where I have my own script of
opinions.

When I am sad I love indulging in sweet sticky cakes.
Come on let's be *united*, it is fine if we are exhausted.
Day by day, I am getting older.

As my world blossoms, my heart roars as loud as a brave lion.
Life can sometimes be unfair!
However, I am ready to take on the storms, the good with the bad, I know I need to be ready to fight the monsters that hide under my bed.
I will let the colours paint my bright future and enjoy playing till I am rolling in laughter.
Until then I will carry on running wild, watching cartoons and enjoying teddy bear cuddles.
I am getting older.

Sahaj Mehta (9)

Buckingham Preparatory School, Pinner

This Is Me!

Everyone is special and unique in their own way,
We all have a right to stand up and say:
"This is what I'm meant to be,
This is me!"

I love football and I control the field,
But I'm not great at fighting with a shield.
I'm mostly happy, sometimes sad
But I always know when I'm good or bad!

Maths and English bring out my finest hour,
Geography makes my tongue go sour.
Music and drama are what I like,
I'm always ready for a good old hike.

Life has taken me places,
Leaving behind memories and familiar faces.
India is my home nation,
But England has given me a new sensation.

In Mumbai, I lived facing the seashore,
With Rhea living next door.

We used to have lots of fun,
Along with Anshu and Hrishi in the sun.

In London now, I live in an apartment block,
Without a single sandy rock.
But I am surrounded by greenery,
And life here's a different scenery.

I make friends wherever I go,
Age no factor, never has been, no, no, no!
Adapting to change comes naturally to me
Whatever be the situation, I manage it with glee.

I am what I am because of my family,
friends, teachers and the world around me!
I know I will continue to evolve
But it will still be *me* and that is what I'm meant to
be!

Vivan Sen (9)

Buckingham Preparatory School, Pinner

If I Could Just Be Me... Well, I Already Am!

If I could just be me, I'd work together as one team with the world.
If I could just be me, I would give humanity anything they need to live in happiness.
If I could just be me, I would cover the seas in Tipp-Ex and have clear oceans.

If I could just be me, I'd smash cricket and my Nintendo together to make my ultimate dream.
If I could just be me, I'd store Big Ben in my belly button so that I never have to worry about time again.
If I could just be me, my hands would be ready to bake cakes smothered gently with white, soft, cotton cream.

If I could just be me, I would swim for miles and miles under the sea, glaring at the nature it owns.
If I could just be me, I'd have my neck as long as a rocket so that I can help myself to a galaxy.
If I could just be me, my tongue would want more of any sweet, especially Skittles so that it could taste the rainbow.

If I could just be me, I would smell pizza from a mile away as it would roar out deafeningly to me.
If I could just be me, I'd keep the London Eye in my eye so that I can visualise all the people I love in my eyeball.
If I could just be me, I would make algebra methods nightmares because maths methods are always easy to forget.

Here I am, head to toe.

Jay Patel (9)
Buckingham Preparatory School, Pinner

It's Me

My thoughts are like
The numerous playful waves,
Soaring and calming down
Like the retreating rays.
My aura is like
The rising sun,
Brings hope and spreads
Brilliance to everyone.
My ambitions keep
Towering by the day,
To be an 'architect'
Is my dream job today.
My Lego toys help me
To develop my skill,
And every piece I assemble
Escalates my will.
To create a marvel
With my Lego toys,
That will bring in me
A smile and loads of joy.

I then place my
Bonsai plants all around,
To create scenic beauty
And absorb the polluting sound.
By all means, I am a
Foodie through and through.
Sharing is caring is
What I always prove.
I have countless friends
And foes are none,
For I love to live life
With frolic and fun.
Sing your heart out
Is what I believe,
Love everyone, create peace
For nobody should grieve.
I wish I could be the silver lining
In the cloud for a while,
And enchant everyone
With my enduring smile.

Shiv Nair (9)
Buckingham Preparatory School, Pinner

My Scar On My Head

The scar on my head I never knew I had,
"It's big!" said Mum one day in a tender voice.
I never knew it was so bad,
Until she told me of the special scar,
That spread across my head,
In a line from ear to ear.

The scar on my head I never knew I had,
Was as long as a 15cm ruler,
Making my head grow now in a normal, common way.
I was only a baby when the scar appeared,
It was small but grew as did I.
Now I love it, it tells my story,
Of what I endured and the battle I won.

The scar on my head, I never knew I had,
It came with a funny name
Saggital Craniosynostosis
It made my head peculiar and my brain squishy,
The doctors at Great Ormond Street, saved my life
I was only small and have no memory,

But I will always love it, as it tells my story,
The scar on my head I never knew I had.

Angad Singh Mahey (9)

Buckingham Preparatory School, Pinner

Happiness Is Me!

H appiness is my favourite emotion,
A nd a chocolate milkshake is my magic potion.
P resents, pens and prizes fill me with merriment,
P astel colouring paper smoothly ignites my enjoyment.
I love cars - the logos and the statistics - they make me grin,
N ice, noble dogs make me want to pet their furry skin.
E very time I meet my friends, my mouth curves into a U.
S cience experiments blow my mind away. *Phew!*
S ums are some of my most favourite things to do.

I like reading books for as long as I am awake,
S topping only to take a toilet break.

M ac 'n' cheese brings cheers to my tummy,
E very day in every way, I feel happiness is me!

Anirvinn Sudarshan (9)

Buckingham Preparatory School, Pinner

If I Were...

If I were a jewel,

I would be a precious diamond that shines so brightly and its rays twinkle in all angles.

If I were an animal,

I would be a wolf who is highly intelligent, caring and travels in a pack like a group of warriors on a mission.

If I were a dinosaur,

I would be a Predator-X because it is the biggest and strongest sea creature ever to live.

If I were water,

I would fill myself up in a stream that flows so gently, with ripples so soft and providing the calm that we all need.

If I were a tool,

I would be a circular saw, so precise, so strong and powerful.

If I were an instrument,

I would be a violin which produces a soothing sound but most importantly it needs a talented violinist to play it.

Perhaps this gives you a glimpse of me...

Shiven Khatri (9)

Buckingham Preparatory School, Pinner

Do You Know The Boy?

Do know the boy who spreads joy and laughter?
Loves his sports, football in the morning and cricket after.
Makes new friends and keeps in touch with pals and a mate,
Tries his best every day to reach school without being late.
Travel is his passion, mountains, villages or sandy seashore,
Burger, pizza, ice cream, enjoys food galore.

Do know the boy who dreams to grow up as a brave soldier?
With proud stars shining on the uniform on his shoulder.
When spring sky has his favourite colour, flowers every corner,
Wishes to cherish moments with family, with his piano and guitar.
Born in India, toddler in Singapore, growing up in London,
Friends call me by many names; the best is when my parents call me 'Hridaan'!

Adrit Basu (9)
Buckingham Preparatory School, Pinner

This Is Ethan

T his is me
H appy things make me feel excited
I don't like cricket or fizzy drinks
S pending time with my cousins is fun

I love football the best
S ports are my favourite (but not all sports)

M edals make me proud
E arning achievements makes me feel impressed
  like a person successfully answered a question

E veryone says that I am energetic
T rick or treating is my favourite thing to do every
  year
H ockey is not my favourite sport
A musement parks are the best
N ever give up, I will keep trying.

Ethan Cheung (9)
Buckingham Preparatory School, Pinner

Likes And Dislikes

L oving supercars is my passion
I love computers and robots in action
K indness is what I like
E njoying riding on a nice sunny day on my bike
S crumptious delicacies make my heart jump with joy.

D on't like the pain in my ears when air pressure drops in a flight
I dislike creepy-crawlies and jump with a fright
S low is what I hate
L ike everybody hates being late
I cannot stand people not being fair
K ind of people who swear
E veryone dislikes a sad ending
S o this is a poem that says all about *me!*

Nikhil Nair
Buckingham Preparatory School, Pinner

Who Am I? What Am I? Well, This Is Me

I'm a chirping bird full of happiness and glee
Singing charming songs all about me.
My coco-coloured skin dazzles in the light and my
favourite time of day is when I rise to shine.
I am a coin tossed heads or tails, day or night,
winning or losing, it will never stop me from
keeping on going.
I'm a cheetah, a quick thinker, fast eater and the
best racer.
Life is a blast being fast!
I'm a silhouette,
A diamond stealer, emerald nicker and ruby
whipper.
The night sky beams, it is my fellow friend, the one
that will never end.
The night sky says, "He's a nicker of a whipper."

This is me, to make most of what life can be.

Om Uday Irniraya (9)
Buckingham Preparatory School, Pinner

If I Could...

If I could fly
I would touch the clear blue sky
Steal the cotton candy clouds
Whilst the birds fly high.

If I could disappear
I would use my senses just to hear
Happy sounds of laughter
Around the world hereafter.

If I could shrink myself
I would talk to the creatures underground
I would listen to the folk tales
Of their plights under the mounds.

If I could turn back the hands of time
I would relive memories of the past
Cherishing the magnificent moments
And hope for them to always last.

If I could have super strength
I would lift the world and shake off all the darkness

Allowing the colours of the rainbow
To leave their mark.

Aarav Patel (9)

Buckingham Preparatory School, Pinner

I Am Ayaansh

God is really creative,
Feel me when you read me.

Crafty, creative and charismatic,
Loves the beat of the music,
Enjoys the divine nature to the fullest,
God made me naughty but cutest.

Inhale positivity from others,
Exhale respect for the elders,
My heart bellowed for the destitute,
The royal game helps me soothe.

As wise as an elf,
I am a shining jewel,
Who wants to touch the magical sky
Lightning Kid is my inspiration to fly.

Became author at the age of seven,
I felt like I was in heaven,
My rainbow heart is full of life,
Reading poems brings smiles.

Last but not the least, this is me,
A precious gift of God, so unique.

Ayaansh Singhal (8)

Buckingham Preparatory School, Pinner

Six Ways To Look At Me!

I am a shining star, home to crazy cricket, cool
chess, a brilliant brain and great gaming,
I am a leaf of a tree, my friends, family and elders
are always by my side seeking to make me the
best I can be,
I am a fighter never letting loss come home and
when it does, I cry thinking I haven't done my job
that I was assigned and can do,
I am a jack-in-the-box, talking, jumping and moving
around the house, throwing a ball onto the wall
like a bowling machine,
I am a ball made of foil making weird noises like
bing! Bing! Bong! Bong!
I say "Today's my day to shine!"

Krishang Upadhyay (9)
Buckingham Preparatory School, Pinner

Fantastic Me!

Playing and watching TV
Is where you'll find me.
I am active, funny and kind.
But be warned, I have a dark side.

My parents won't let me have a pet
Because they think that they are smelly and wet!
My parents are still the best
As they beat all the rest.

I love eating sweets.
But my parents say they are treats.
I love making Lego builds.
And I have become very skilled.
Football is my favourite sport.
Sometimes, I have thoughts
What if I made it to pro.
I would make lots of dough!

So, this is fantastic me!
And I am happy to be me!

Dhilan Joshi (9)
Buckingham Preparatory School, Pinner

What's In A Name?

M odest, thoughtful, amiable and kind-hearted, that's me

U nbreakable is the bond with my family

H ope is the bird song that awakens me with a smile

A lways will I succeed, even if pain it needs

M asterful, innovative Lego creator

M ature like an ancient temple

A ngered by poverty, injustice and racial enmity

D eep in my heart gushes a spring of love for all humanity.

Muhammad Al-Mahdi Esmail (9)

Buckingham Preparatory School, Pinner

I Am Kamil

K ind and caring,
A s adventurous as an ape.
M ighty and magnificent,
I mpassioned and intensive,
L oyal and lively like a leopard.

P oetic and peaceful,
O pen-minded and observant,
C alm and cheerful,
I nnovative and ingenious,
A s amazing and awe-inspiring as an aardvark.
S elf-reliant and smart. I am
K amil!

Kamil Pociask (8)
Buckingham Preparatory School, Pinner

I Am Kyle

I am 9 years old

When I am swimming I glide like a shark fin

When I am dancing I move like the wind

When I am sleeping I am quiet as a mouse, *shhhhhhhh*

When I am singing my voice goes high-pitched

When I am angry my eyes rage red as blood and fists go tight... deep sighhh

When I am happy, I am excited just like the sun.

Kyle Toussaint-Gyampo (9)

Buckingham Preparatory School, Pinner

Sanctuary

Lost lanes
Seeking safety
All alone
Escaping war
Lost homes
Needing rest
Travelling times
Always war
Places wrecked
Always looking
Never resting
Surviving war
Finding hope
Finding love
Sanctuary.

Lacey
Byker Primary School, Byker

Sanctuary

Lost homes
Always roams
Escapes home
Loud tone
Home searching
Always lurking
Can walk
Can talk
Torn inside
Fine outside
Weak inside
Strong outside
Home seeking
Safety reaching
Tears leaking
People hating
Refugees debating
People try
Refugees cry
Taking chances

Hunting safety Sanctuary.

Francesca

Byker Primary School, Byker

Sanctuary

Dangerous fighting
Loud bangs
Loud bombs
Children crying
Planes flying
Stop fighting
Help arriving
No fighting
Being safe
Sanctuary.

Muayyad
Byker Primary School, Byker

A Recipe For Me

Ingredients:
1 dash of happiness
A seasoning of rugby
1 drizzle of cricket
1 handful of gaming
A scoop of joy
A sprinkle of kindness

Method:
1. Pre-heat the oven to the year 2012.
2. Grab your Sorting Hat bowl.
3. First add a dash of happiness.
4. Next, pour in one handful of gaming. Heat the Xbox then add to the bowl.
5. Then stir in one drizzle of cricket.
6. Add a scoop full of joy.
7. Stir with a cricket bat and season with rugby.
8. Pour into a colouring pot and bake for 10 years.
9. Take out the oven and leave for 2 months.
10. Finally, add a sprinkle of kindness on top.

There you have it, a George Freeman.

George Freeman (10)
Cawood CE Primary School, Cawood

Inside My Brain

If you opened my brain what would you see?
I'm sometimes happy, I'm sometimes sad.
Is that bad?
I'm happy to have friends that want to play with me.
I'm sad that sometimes it's not always that easy.
I sit and wonder what could I be?
Will I drive a car that goes really far?
Or will my name go down in history?
Will I be a popstar, or open my dream bakery?
Will my family be there to congratulate me?
Being inside my brain can be a kerfuffle.
I'm a warrior, a wanderer, a dreamer, and a believer, which makes me feel so special.
I think it's good to be me.

Elizabeth Dean (9)
Cawood CE Primary School, Cawood

All About Me!

I love to sing, from in my house, to in a cave
I love to play sports, netball is my fave,
I love to bake, it doesn't matter if it doesn't go right
I love to party, sometimes all through the night!

I am loving, persevering and kind
I have a thoughtful, unique, caring mind,
In my world, others always come first
My kindness bubble will never burst!

My hair is silk, so soft and smooth
My cheeks are roses, so fragile and delicate,
My eyes are sapphires, so bright and gleaming
Yes, my whole body is pretty and beautiful!

Holly Hindmarch (10)

Cawood CE Primary School, Cawood

My Life

My name is Megan,
I'm 10 years old,
I like cricket,
And I'm as good as gold.

I love to read,
It makes me smile,
I've got lots of books,
It'll take me a while.

I go to Brownies,
I did a parade,
I work towards badges,
With stuff that I've made.

I like to swim,
I'm in stage six,
I love watching Strictly,
All the kicks and flicks.

Oh, and there's the end of the Megan mix.

Megan Stephenson (10)
Cawood CE Primary School, Cawood

My Life

My life is big,
My life is strong,
I can do right,
I can do wrong.

Wherever I go,
Whatever I do,
I'll always smile,
All the way through.

When life is rough,
I can be tough,
And I'll see it,
All the way through.

This means
My life is big,
Wherever I go,
When life is rough,
I'll smile my way home.

Maisy Vinton (9)
Cawood CE Primary School, Cawood

Recipe For Daniel

To make this you will need:
A pinch of excitement
A spoonful of dodgeball
A cupful of basketball
A drop of skipping
A splash of tennis
A dash of happiness

Give it a mix
Put it in the cool oven because I am cool
And shape it with your friends
Followed by playing with your friends because you get to spend time with your friends.

Daniel Murray (10)
Cawood CE Primary School, Cawood

Who Am I?

A kennings poem

Cat lover
Big hugger
Nature carer
Indoor water competitor
Harry Potter reader
Tilly Ramsey recipe follower
Horse rider
Bake Off watcher
Cornwall surfer
Netball shooter
Mountain climber
Brownie badge achiever
Light sleeper
Salted caramel ice cream eater
Sister teaser
Weekend adventurer.
I'm Amber.

Amber Smales (10)
Cawood CE Primary School, Cawood

What I Love

I love football
I love basketball
I love rugby
I love netball

I love these things
Because if I feel
Down I can think
How talented I am

My dream for the future is to be a basketball player
Imagine all the goals I would score

I am caring,
Kind and friendly.
This is me!

Dylan Davenport (9)
Cawood CE Primary School, Cawood

Myself

My name is Madison
I am 9 years old.
I am loving, helpful, kind and caring.
I want to be a singer when I am older.
I give a warm welcome
And I love dancing.
I like arts and crafts.
I am *always* happy.
My emotions colour who I am
Because I am so *bright!*

Madison Jessop
Cawood CE Primary School, Cawood

Who Am I?

Who am I?
Caring, kind and a bit cheeky.
Who am I?
Loving football and playing with friends.
Who am I?
Wanting to be a policeman.
Who am I?
Loud and very chatty.
Who am I?
This is me!

Charlie Holdcroft (9)
Cawood CE Primary School, Cawood

Doggy

I've got a little dog.
Its name is Betty.
It runs around the garden
And gets warm and sweaty.
So I sat her in the wind to get nice and cool.
She pushed me out of the way
And jumped in the pool.

Alfie Brooke (9)
Cawood CE Primary School, Cawood

My Life

My name is Jonah
And I am eight
I go to Cawood Primary
And I like to do science.

I like to watch The Simpsons
And read Tom Gates
I also do taekwondo
And that is my life.

Jonah Hood (8)
Cawood CE Primary School, Cawood

A Poem About Me

I may not be perfect
But I am still me
I am a girl who
Likes football
Yep, that is me
I dream about football
When I am asleep
I support Leeds United
But I am still me.

Alana Thorpe (10)
Cawood CE Primary School, Cawood

Here's A Poem About Me

Like Marmite, like me or not, that is me.
But I am sensitive and kind,
I can be funny and cheeky.
I am a brown-haired, grey-eyed child.

I'm slow at getting ready,
Because I am way too lazy.
I'm annoyed too much by my siblings,
They drive me crazy.

I have many fears,
And horrible thoughts,
So I like hugs,
To make me feel better.

I am an animal lover,
But giraffes are the best,
Then monkeys, then the cat family,
Then all the rest.

I live in Wellington,
Born in Wolverhampton,

My dad's family comes from Warrington,
The three Ws, wow, wow, wow!

That's the story of me!

Finlay Langard-Brown (10)
Dothill Primary School, Wellington

Springtime And Me

The beautiful blossom
Falls from the trees,
White and pink,
Blows in the breeze.

The sound of birds,
Singing their song,
Morning and night,
And all day long.

I like to play outside,
On my trampoline or swing,
I have a pet bunny,
Who I love stroking.

The sun is shining,
Bright in the sky,
All are blinded,
When meets the eye.

Bees are buzzing,
In the air,

Collecting nectar,
Everywhere.

The flowers are blooming,
The trees grow tall,
Spring is my favourite
Season of all.

Sophia Haycock (10)
Dothill Primary School, Wellington

A Recipe For Me

This will be a recipe for me!
I'll collect the ingredients,
And soon you will see
This is what makes me.

I'll knead the happiness thoroughly,
Add a pinch of laughter there and then
I will pour in the creativity slowly and carefully,
This is what makes me.

Time to add a spoonful of music,
Maybe a drawing or two,
Stir it so it's nice and thick,
This is what makes me.

The last thing is a few friends,
Now bake and leave to set,
My recipe has come to an end,
And it's one especially for me!

Daisy Swales (9)
Dothill Primary School, Wellington

Scared And Alone

Mean comments all around,
As I heard them in my head,
Look at her, haha, haha,
All scared and alone...

Over there with fake friends,
I didn't know she has friends,
Ha, ha, ha, ha, ha...

Over walks a girl,
"Who is that?" they whisper to each other,
Ha, ha, ha, she must be stupid
Not so scared and alone anymore...

Jamie-Leigh Parsons (10)
Dothill Primary School, Wellington

Football

My name's Kayleigh, I am 9,
I like playing all the time.
Playing football is my sport,
Kicking, tackling, scoring goals.
Man United's my favourite team,
Playing for them would be my dream.
Red's the colour of their kit,
On the pitch they all get fit.
Football, football is my thing,
Come on you reds, is what I sing.

Kayleigh Holehouse (9)
Dothill Primary School, Wellington

Harness Your Fire

Harness your fire
Your personality is your attire
Keep your head high
Just be yourself
You're magic like an elf
Your worries and fears will die.

Don't listen to the bullies
They're just being 'dull'ies
Your personality is your attire
Harness your fire
Harness your shining fire.

Franklin Carpenter (10)
Dothill Primary School, Wellington

My Colours

Blue is either sadness or hope,
Yellow is respectfulness and kindness,
Red equals coolness or ferocious power,
Green means boredom or sickness,
Orange means fullness and enthusiasm,
Purple means happiness or being disappointed,
Pink means togetherness,
Black means self-confidence,
White means pureness.

Thomas Olliver (10)
Dothill Primary School, Wellington

All About Faye

I love maths,
Maths is fun,
I'm good at maths,
I love my mum.

I've got four sisters
And six brothers.
The oldest is Chloe,
I've only one mother.

My hobby is martial arts,
My favourite subject is art.
My least favourite is English,
Everybody farts.

Faye Duff (10)
Dothill Primary School, Wellington

All About Me

I am as creative as an artist
My personality is best described as purple
Helpful is my middle name
I bounce around task to task like a rabbit
One of my favourite things to do is read like a
book worm just like Harry Potter
I am as kind as my heart
I have long brown hair as lovely as silk.

Lucie Hayward (9)
Dothill Primary School, Wellington

All About Me

My name is Bella Wall
And I love my football

It keeps me fit and on edge
With the help of my fruit and veg

I also enjoy baking with my mom
Cakes for the family and brother Dom

My family means a lot to me
Also my nan that I often see.

Bella Wall (8)
Dothill Primary School, Wellington

Senses

Music ringing in my head,
The wood,
The string,
A gentle sound.

I see my freckles,
I feel my hair,
I hear my breath,
And close my eyes.

Happy, hungry,
Joyful jumps,
Sometimes hard,
But always fun!

Harriet Archer-Jones (10)
Dothill Primary School, Wellington

My Diverse And Unique Personality

I have black eyes like the night skies...
I am fun yet quiet like a baby panther.
I love learning water safety, spotting dangers in the Navy!
I dream of playing a hockey tournament in a stadium for my team!
My favourite animals are a cobra, a monitor lizard and a Ganges shark with an enormous mark!
I'm as awesome as a superhero who flies through the cloudy skies!
I love video games with beams and racing!
I love singing with my choir and last year I got hired!
This is
My diverse and unique
Personality!

Glenn Tong (7)
Faraday School, Poplar

Curiosity

As quiet as a shy mouse
My brain is burning on fire
I'm as curious as a junior scientist
As fast as the speed of sound
As smart as a physics professor
I'm as fun as a parrot
I hate the sound of screeches
But like computing very much
I'm as awesome as a superhero
That flies through the sky
I may not seem active but I am
Because this is me.

Ishaan Sutaria (7)
Faraday School, Poplar

Cooking Myself

First, let's start to make the dough...
Let's pour a half of love to make it sweet as pie.
Then get a spoon of beauty as beautiful as a swan.
Put in dark chocolate as dark as my hair.
Then add a whole chunk of my heart...
Now that you have cooked, spread in your part!
My eyes are as black as blackberries.
I am as sweet as a cupcake.
This is me!

Ira Kishore (8)

Faraday School, Poplar

As Silly As A Banana

This is me,
I am fun yet friendly,
I am confident and crafty,
I am loving as a lizard,
I am as beautiful as a big brown bear!
My eyes are as blue as a lagoon,
My hair is as blonde as a bright star,
My lips are as rosy red as a ruby,
I love bananas, you will find me most silly!
I'm a silly banana, a silly banana am I...

Emerson Krasilnick (8)
Faraday School, Poplar

The Chilled, Sporty, Friendly Child

I am Akshay.
I am as brave as a lion.
My eyes are as brown as chocolate shining.
I am fearless as a ferocious fighting fox.
My brain grows rapidly every day.
I am as smart as an educator.
But most importantly I try my best,
Even if I am losing a match or something.
I am chilled, sporty and friendly
Yet so passionate.

Akshay Siddharth (8)
Faraday School, Poplar

I'm As Fast As A Cheetah

I'm as fast as a cheetah
I'm as funny as a flamingo
I'm as smart as a scientist
My favourite colour is burning flame blue
I'm artistic as an ant
I hate pink, purple, unicorns, mermaids and
magical things
My skin is as dark as caramel
My hair is as dark as chocolate
It's blackish brown
This is me!

Chidinma Blackwell (8)
Faraday School, Poplar

Creature Royale

This is me; I'm as adventurous as a fun monkey!
This is me; I'm as silly as a red clown!
This is me; I'm as curious as a newborn cat!
This is me; I'm as messy as a pug.
This is me; I'm as chilled as a sleeping sloth...
This is me; I'm as happy as a squirrel with a nut.
This is me!

Alfie Hobbs (8)

Faraday School, Poplar

I'm As Happy As An Exploding Firework

I love building and coding as much as a robot.
I'm as happy as an exploding firework!
I am as brave as a lion.
I'm as sporty as a flying fox.
I'm as strong as a tree.
My eyes are as golden as a setting sun.
I'm as friendly as a poodle.
I'm as fast as a cheetah.
This is me!

Benjamin Whatling (7)

Faraday School, Poplar

I Am As Fearless As A Fierce, Feathered Phoenix

I am as curious as a kitten.
I am as adventurous as a dolphin.
I am as fearless as a fierce, feathered phoenix.
I am as fast as a peregrine falcon.
I climb as well as lightning strikes!
I swim like a slithering sea serpent.
I am as athletic as a spider monkey.
This is my personality!

Oscar Ramsbottom (7)
Faraday School, Poplar

The Silly, Shimmering Space Artist

I am fun,
I am as artistic as Picasso,
I am adventurous,
My hair is as dark as dark chocolate,
My eyes are as shimmering as stars,
But most importantly I am as kind and as beautiful as the sun!
But don't forget I shine at sports,
This is the wonderful Sienna!

Sienna Lodhia (7)
Faraday School, Poplar

My Life And I

I'm as funny as a laughing cheetah!
I'm passionate about animals
I'm as wise as a hooting owl
My eyes are as dark as dirt
I'm as fearless as a fighting warrior
I hate Velcro noises and girly stuff
This is my life and I.

Theia Kothari (7)

Faraday School, Poplar

Eyes As Blue As Two Sapphires

I'm as skilled as an Olympic climber!
I'm as silly as a clown!
I can swim as well as a mermaid!
I can dance as well as Darcey Bussell!
I don't like people shouting at me!
My eyes are as blue as two sapphires!
This is me!

Isabelle Clancy (7)
Faraday School, Poplar

Who Am I?

I am as curious as a cat.
I am a maths wizard and I like money!
I am as friendly as a fairy.
I am as brave as a lion.
I am as awesome as a god.
I am as cool as a cobra.
I am as fast as a jaguar!

This is me!

Jagger Hou (8)
Faraday School, Poplar

As Friendly As A Poodle

I'm as friendly as a poodle
I'm as bright as a firework
I'm as strong as a tree
I'm as silly as a clown
I'm as fast as a car
My eyes are as golden as the shimmering sunset.
This is me.

Banner Thorne (7)
Faraday School, Poplar

As Awesome As An Alien

My eyes are as shiny as the stars
I'm as friendly and fun as a poodle
I'm as artistic as Monet
This is me...
I'm as silly as a crazy clown
I'm as awesome as an alien.
This is me!

Dixie Pittuck (8)
Faraday School, Poplar

As Artistic As Joseph Vernet

I am as fun as a game and as friendly as a poodle
I am as smart as a laptop yet I hate the ring of fire drills
My eyes are as blue as lapis lazuli
I am as artistic as Joseph Vernet
This makes me!

Owen Blanchandin (8)
Faraday School, Poplar

Inside Me

I am Isabella.
I am as smart as a robot.
I'm as chilled as a cucumber.
I am passionate about hamsters.
My eyes are as brown as chocolate.

Isabella Chen (7)
Faraday School, Poplar

Famous Fred

My name is Freddie and I'll soon be on your telly
I'm sure these words will make you wiggle like jelly!

I'm a tidy boy but I control the ball like Messi
On the pitch I'm hefty, I score goals with my lefty!

They be like "Oh! There's Freddie on my telly!"
Famous prince, pass me my crown!

Try to get past me, I will take that boy down!
I megged him! I will take that boy down!

Everybody buys tickets when Freddie's around!

Freddie Williams (11)
New Rush Hall School, Ilford

This Is Tillie

T his is who I am
H appy and friendly
I nventive and creative
S ort of fast

I 'm a good friend
S neaky and fun

M e, it's just me and I'm amazing
E nd of poem, I wouldn't want to be anyone else!

Tillie Follen (11)
New Rush Hall School, Ilford

Things

People are different,
So why do people bully people for who they are?
Like... you get bananas
One is mashed
You think it is disgusting but
Another person thinks it is delicious!
But you be rude about it
And get in trouble for it
What I'm saying is
Leave people
So you don't get in trouble.

Phillip Hurst (10)
New Rush Hall School, Ilford

Me

I am angry, feisty and everything nasty
I'm always lookin' grumpy but it doesn't look nasty
I'm stubborn all the time and don't get paid a dime
That's just me
And if you don't wanna see
Then that's fine
It's just an opinion of mine.

Marcus Rolston-Jones (11)
New Rush Hall School, Ilford

Animals

I am I and I like animals
They calm me down
Not make me frown
They're tricky and mischievous
And all things devious
And I think...
They're very cute.

Sidney Turvey (11)
New Rush Hall School, Ilford

I Love...

I love my best friends, they always make me laugh,
I love sleep and I love having a nap,
I love listening to music, it has a hold on me,
I love David Bowie, although Blackstar makes me weep,
I love Cornwall, I wish I were there every week,
I love Marvel, it makes me laugh until I'm weak,
I love Tyler, the Creator and I love his technique,
I love Canada, I think about it when I sleep,
But most importantly, I love my dog and I never want her to leave.

Isabel Walsh (11)
Northcote Primary School, Liverpool

Liverpool

L eague cups, we've won nine
I nvincible, we're the best
V an Dijk, the world's best centre back
E verton Vs Liverpool, so exciting
R afael Benítez - a Liverpool legend
P remier League
O n the field we're great
O ff the field we show love and respect
L eague titles, twenty

F A cups, eight, wow!
C hampions League, six.

Jake Cashen (11)

Northcote Primary School, Liverpool

My Subject

I'm delighted when I do hard maths questions
But I don't mind doing easy ones to focus more on
little mistakes
Maths makes me feel calm and happy
But I can just relax while doing maths
Because it's like I'm at a birthday party
This is so helpful for me
To sit down and relax
The sum of this book is lovely
I want to read it again
The equation of life is so hard to learn.

Luke Tillman (11)

Northcote Primary School, Liverpool

Champions League Winners

The Champions League trophy
Sitting proud and tall
I wish it would come to me whenever I call
As I step onto the pitch, I hope I don't fall
Ninety minutes later, the trophy is ours
The streets are painted red
People cheering overhead
I can hardly sleep as I crawl into bed
What a night it has been
But it was worth it because
Liverpool are the winners of the Champions League.

Raimi Nigel Bature (10)

Northcote Primary School, Liverpool

All About Me

I am a nine-year-old girl
I have big blue eyes
And long blonde curls
I really like to be outside with the blue skies.

I really enjoy gymnastics
I am a good swimmer
Sport is actually fantastic
But I really enjoy my dinner!

Playing with my friends is fun
We can be a little bit crazy
But when all is done
I'm just me, Lacey!

Lacey Matthews (9)
Northcote Primary School, Liverpool

When I'm Tired

When I'm tired I start to fall asleep.
As I drift into another world I begin to leap.
Leap through all the dandelions and the daisies too!
Oh, what a world this is, I hope I don't get the flu!
I twirl and whirl through the clouds, happy as can be.
I wake up energised and free.
Oh, what a world this is.
I can now go to the farm and see some pigs.

Kaitlyn Hamilton-Graney (10)
Northcote Primary School, Liverpool

My Dog, Princess

She is always a ray of sunshine
When she smiles, she brightens my day
Her teeth are whiter than the sun
She puts her little black nose in my ear
It makes me cry with laughter
I take her to the park
She thinks she's bigger than other dogs
She's always there for me when I am upset
Or I have a bad day
She's my best friend.

Halle Dwyer (9)
Northcote Primary School, Liverpool

Anger

Anger is a bit like a monster,
Who hides deep inside,
And builds up a strong emotion,
That washes up like a tide.

Anger can get the better of us,
Anger can also make us sad,
Anger can isolate us,
Make us feel bad.

Anger is a feeling
No one can avoid,
Anger is a feeling
That's never left unemployed.

Niamh Brown (11)
Northcote Primary School, Liverpool

Halloween

H alloween is spooky
A time for fear
L ooking at the terrifying pumpkins
L ollipops are yummy
O rderly fashion, we trick or treat one by one
W ishing I could have a friend
E arns money all the time
E lders are annoyed every day
N amed my rabbit on Halloween.

Luca Evason (10)

Northcote Primary School, Liverpool

Sadness

Every day,
Every hour,
Every minute,
Every second,
I feel emptiness, low, lost, glum
When I'm sad I feel sick, distressed
Like nobody is there for me
Blue is all I see
I try and hide my sadness
And if I don't then I will just hurt people's feelings
Sadness is all I feel...

Jennifer Boyd Clarke (11)
Northcote Primary School, Liverpool

Holiday

H appiness is good
O f course you are the best person ever
L et's just not give up
I t's just so nice meeting friends
D oing new things
A lways follow your dreams
Y ou are the best person ever - you're the one
who made me the better person.

Archie Willis (11)

Northcote Primary School, Liverpool

These Emotions

I am surprised when I get presents for my birthday
I feel angry when my brother shouts at me
I am confident when I get motivation from friends
and family
I am sorry when I say things I don't mean
I am happy when I get to play with my dogs
I feel loved when I spend time with family and
friends.

Lyla Jaycock Fury (10)
Northcote Primary School, Liverpool

Poem Name No One Ever Thought Of

Christmas can be cool,
And autumn is astounding.

But birthdays are bad in my book,
Films are futile,
And chocolate may be corrosive.

But my family are friendly and funny,
And bread is better with butter or PB.

And these are all the things
That
Make
Me!

Adrian Burca (11)
Northcote Primary School, Liverpool

All About Me

I am nine years old
I like the cold
I support Liverpool
I like the pool

I play football
I don't like to fall
I like apple juice
I also like chocolate mousse

My favourite subject is maths
I walk on the path
I love my mother
I respect my brother.

Chloe Jones (9)
Northcote Primary School, Liverpool

Do What's Best For You

Most people like the way I am,
I like the way I am,
Friends make you who you are,
They are the start of your life,
Sometimes don't trust your friends,
People can't change who you are,
Don't let them tell you what's best,
It's all on your life choices.

Freddie Baxter (10)
Northcote Primary School, Liverpool

Joseph

B eautiful newborn baby
A fter nine months
B orn on the 10th of May
Y ay!

J oseph
O n the hospital bed
S o cute and happy
E very day I waited for him
P erfect little angel
H e is Joseph.

Daniel Elliott (11)
Northcote Primary School, Liverpool

Rainbows

R ain in the sky

A person you are

I n my heart you will stay

N an, you are never forgotten

B ows and arrows right through my heart

O ur lord in the sky

W ill he take you but you stay in a secret place?

S ee you soon.

Aleisha Robinson (11)

Northcote Primary School, Liverpool

Emotions

E very emotion is different
M ine are too
O ther people react differently
T hough we still have emotions
I can't explain mine
O verwhelmed all the time
N o one reacts the same
S o why should we act the same?

Macy Parkin (10)
Northcote Primary School, Liverpool

My Favourite Game

I love this sport so much,
It's so fun,
I want to play all day but my mum stops me to
take a break,
I watch my favourite team all day
And I want to be like them one day,
That's my goal,
One day to stand on my feet
And play the game.

Mateo Kulli (11)
Northcote Primary School, Liverpool

Delightful Daisy

She likes playing with her friends
She's a bubbly, beautiful soul
She loves making others laugh
She loves helping others
She always makes sure others are okay
Even if she is not
She wears a bow as bright as a daisy.

Daisy Rose McKibbin (10)

Northcote Primary School, Liverpool

Litter Land

Litter, litter everywhere
Even more litter than hair
It starts off small then piles up
Even bigger than all the books
Litter on the streets starts to reek
Even on the beach
So clean up your street
Before the heat.

Poppy-Jo Fairclough (8)
Northcote Primary School, Liverpool

Laughter

Laughter comes out to play when someone tells a joke
He loves to smile and brighten everyone's day
But when no one is there to tell him a joke
He gets bored and goes away until the day
When he can come and play again.

Peyton Cliffe (10)
Northcote Primary School, Liverpool

Happy

Happy is like a ray of sunshine, it brightens up your
day
Happy is a feeling that makes sadness go away
Happy is an emotion that comes out
When you play with your friends and when you
laugh
Happy is worth more than money.

Mia O'Brien (10)

Northcote Primary School, Liverpool

Boxing

B oxing takes my anger away
O n my chest is gloves after getting hit
X -rays after X-rays
I n the ring day after day
N ever not in the ring
G oing there is the hardest part.

Jaeden Bloxham (11)
Northcote Primary School, Liverpool

Rudy's Life

I am cool
But I don't have a pool
I am good at football
You better make a footstool

I am not bad
I'm just not a hard lad
I'm the best
That's why I've gotta go rest.

Rudy Iurcia (10)

Northcote Primary School, Liverpool

Smudge's Journey

This all started when my mum found a cat
And we named him Smudge
He can be a bit of a terror
He will get your feet before bed
He will hide from the other kids, except one... me!

Jason Ian Evans (10)
Northcote Primary School, Liverpool

All About The Amazing Me

M y friends
I nseparable from Jasmine
L oves art
L oving and caring
I n love with Netflix
E legant.

Millie Smith-Stoddern (10)
Northcote Primary School, Liverpool

Heidi's Idea

H appiness is in the air
E veryone is equal
I see good in you
D on't give up
I have an idea.

Heidi Lindop (11)
Northcote Primary School, Liverpool

Holiday

When a holiday is near,
I start to cheer,
In the plane,
There is no more rain,
When I'm there,
Freedom is in the air.

Estelle Lucia Fernandez (11)
Northcote Primary School, Liverpool

Riddle Me This

You fall over
And you cry
You hit your toe
In the middle of the night
What you feel
Is pain.

Will Henry Cain (11)

Northcote Primary School, Liverpool

All About Me

I like fairies and magic and the colour pink
I have a black and white dog but he always stinks
I have blue eyes that appear lighter in the sun
I find gymnastics really really fun
I love to do my make-up, especially for a party
My favourite chocolate out of them all is one
hundred per cent Smarties
I like sunny days when I get to ride my bike
But when I have to run I've started to dislike
Now you know a little bit about me
I hope this makes you very happy
Goodbye friend, I hope you have a nice day,
Or as a fairy would say, "I'm going to fly fly away."

Jessica Ball (9)

Our Lady Mother Of The Saviour Catholic Primary School,
Palacefields

The Poem About Me

My name is Oscar, it begins with an O
My last name is Evans, it begins with an E
If you don't know about me
I like to play on my PlayStation on my favourite
game
I like to cook and make yummy foods
I like going to the safari park and stroking all the
animals
But most of all I like to be in school
I like the puzzles, quizzes and maths
So if you don't know that about me
Now you know a little about me.

Oscar Evans (7)
Our Lady Mother Of The Saviour Catholic Primary School,
Palacefields

Springtime

S unflower seeds rising in the big, bright sun
P erfect pink and purple pansies lighting fields up
R ed roses are back and also healthy
I nsects flying through the crisp sky
N ever been happier in the bright springtime
G ive the new flowers a welcome and a dream.

Lily Mayock (9)

Our Lady Mother Of The Saviour Catholic Primary School,
Palacefields

Football Team

I am Imaamah and I like to play football
Football is my passion
Football is what I do
I want to play in a team
Football is my dream
My dad is my coach
And he is my support
Sport is in my heart
I know I am smart
I love a jam tart
Football is my art
My little brother is my sweetheart.

Imaamah Khan (9)
Parkwood Primary School, Keighley

Zakkary

Z akkary is an energetic eight-year-old boy
A pple is his favourite fruit
K icking a ball up high
K eeping it close to him
A s fast as a zebra
R ummaging through the cupboards for the biscuits
Y elling at his games.

Zakkary Harris (8)
Parkwood Primary School, Keighley

This Is Me

I may not be Princess Aurora
But I am always a little princess to my dad
I may not be an angel Gabriel
But I am a cute little angel for my mum
I may not be the best helper
But I am a loving sister to my brother.

Maanya Sathish (7)
Parkwood Primary School, Keighley

Family

I love my family
They are always kind
They treat me like a princess
But sometimes they embarrass me.

Konni Bland-Farmery (9)

Parkwood Primary School, Keighley

This Is Me

This is me, and I adore myself.
But I think I've got something, I can tell.

I like to eat, sleep, work and play.
But that would be way too boring to say!

I do enjoy some chicken nuggets
Because let's be serious now, who doesn't?

This is me, and I adore myself.
But I think I've got something, I can tell.

I can only sleep with teddy bears,
If you take them away, then I'll be scared.

I like to dream when I close my eyes,
And in the morning I can arise.

This is me, and I adore myself.
But I think I've got something, I can tell.

When I get my brain in gear and go to school
I work really hard, and try to improve.

Two years ago I had just moved,
I've learned from then, to impress and improve.

This is me, and I adore myself.
But I think I've got something, I can tell.

I love to play, it is so fun
But I can't do it all day, especially in the sun!

This is me, and I adore myself.
But I think I've got something, I can tell.

I'm really happy that you've read my rhymes,
But before you go, just take your time
To appreciate such good rhymes,
But I bet that yours ain't better than mine!

Mylena Mboungo Guewo (9)
St Brigid's Primary School, Northfield

This Is Me

If you can see a football rolling, I won't be far
behind.
Football is in everything I do, even in my mind.

I love to score, tackle and dribble.
I play all over the pitch, but mainly in the middle.

My main team are claret and blue.
You can often hear me shouting,
"Suuuuuuuuuuuuuuuuu!"

My favourite player is Grealish, but he left for
another team.
As a footballer myself, I understand you need to
follow your dreams.

Someday I hope to be in my claret and blue
heaven,
For my parents to hear over the tannoy...

"Goal scored by Alfie Huggins, Villa's number 7!"

Alfie Huggins (10)
St Brigid's Primary School, Northfield

Simply Me

I like to eat grapes, corn and peas,
My favourite snack is macaroni cheese.
I'm full of joy and I'm as happy as can be,
I'm always very busy, busy as a bee!
Nature is beautiful, the world is great,
I'm learning Albanian on Google Translate!
I love the colours purple, green and red too,
My brother's favourite colour is satin sky-blue.
I love to bounce on my green trampoline
But swimming in the Olympics would be my
future dream.
I've so much love thanks to my big family tree,
They remind me I'm special for just simply
being me!

Ava Djali (8)
St Brigid's Primary School, Northfield

This Is Me

My name is Hugo,
I'm nine years old,
I have a way with words,
Or so I've been told.

I'm naturally curious
And love to explore,
Climbing trees and wildlife adventures,
Birds and little bugs are hard to ignore.

I love to game,
Pokémon is my fave,
Winning battles,
The bravest of the brave!

Using imagination,
I often sit and draw,
Creating new characters
Is what I adore.

I can be sensitive and a little shy,
But once I get to know you,

We'll have lots of laughs
And our worries will be few.

Hugo Snelgrove-Thompson (9)

St Brigid's Primary School, Northfield

This Is Me

Hi, this is me
You are not me
She is not me
He is not me

You are you
I am not you
She is not you
He is not you

My favourite colour is blue
And you're gonna do what you want to do
They might wanna learn to play the flute
And we're gonna give negativity the boot

When your mind says
Blend in with the other kids
Or
Don't be different
Just say,
"This is me
I am unique

I'm not an antique
I ain't afraid to speak!"

This is me
I love the way I speak
I love the way I look
I'm anything but weak

This is me.

Isabel Stephen (10)
St Brigid's Primary School, Northfield

This Is Me, Rachel D

I am a unique, studying, dancing girl,
Who thinks reading is as precious as a pearl.
I love my family
And I am very friendly.
I adore flowers, especially tulips
And I enjoy going on school trips.
I enjoy listening to music
And I like to do a dancing trick.
My favourite season is autumn,
The rich colours are full of optimism.

My name is Rachel,
Some people say I act like an angel.
I dislike asparagus,
It tastes quite suspicious.

Rachel D (9)
St Brigid's Primary School, Northfield

Why Bella Means Beautiful

I'm here to let you understand
That I'm your storyteller,
With skin as golden as the sand,
Hello, my name is Bella.

With emerald eyes and wavy hair,
I'm loyal, fair and calm.
There's no one else you can compare,
I will never cause you harm.

They say that I am quite mature
And sensible and kind.
I'm sure that is what friends are for,
Good friends are hard to find.

Bella Fryer (9)
St Brigid's Primary School, Northfield

All About Me

Hi, my name is Elyam
I'm kind and helpful
I'm as fast as a cheetah
And I like to play football.

Monday to Friday
I go to school
Whenever I go there
I feel very cool.

My hobby is reading
It's really amazing
Mrs Perry once told me
It's kind of like dreaming.

I am good as you can see
That's why I love everything about me!

Elyam Teklit (9)
St Brigid's Primary School, Northfield

This Is Me

I want to be an architect,
Because of my intellect.

I am proud of always trying my best,
Sometimes, I realise I need to rest.

I do a lot of things bit by bit,
And if I can't do something, I will never quit.

I am proud of what I've done,
Oh, let me tell you, there have been a ton.

I have lots of talents,
Therefore I am gallant.

I always smile with glee,
That's me!

Amarise Anyaorah (10)
St Brigid's Primary School, Northfield

This Is Me

This is me, I like to create things.
Sometimes it feels like a gate to King's.

By this I mean it feels great.
Sometimes it's a piece of cake.

Sushi and ramen are my favourite food
And I don't like it when people are rude.

My dream is to be an excellent architect
Maybe it will have an effect.
Things that I like others may not,
Like eating chillies that are very hot!

Lukas Tylenis (10)
St Brigid's Primary School, Northfield

This Is Me

I sabelle is my name, poetry is my game.

S elfless am I,

A pproachable to those who are shy.

B rave as can be,

E lated when I get chilli for tea.

L ikeable and loveable,

L aughing with my friends,

E very day at St Brigid's is great, I hope it never ends.

Isabelle Pritchard (8)

St Brigid's Primary School, Northfield

This Is Me

Tricks by my little white dog, Coco,
Happy with my cute fluffy dog,
In the house my dog follows my dad,
So Dad will play with him.

I like to play with Coco too
But sometimes he barks too much
And my dad gets annoyed.

Each day is fun with my dog
Named after Coco Pops!

Hayley Muirhead (8)
St Margaret Of Scotland Primary School, South Carbrian

This Is Me

T ime after time playing my Xbox,
H appy fun time,
I never play ice hockey,
S uper researcher in my class.

I like my Batman toy,
S liding down the chute.

M y hair looks gold like the sun,
E very day Studyladder is easy for me!

Charlie Smellie (8)

St Margaret Of Scotland Primary School, South Carbrian

This Is Me

T his is the best day ever,
H appy as can be,
I like the laptop,
S amara-Hope is a champion on the laptop.

I ce cream is my creamy favourite,
S chool is the best.

M y new school will be so fun,
E veryone likes me!

Samara-Hope O'Connor (7)
St Margaret Of Scotland Primary School, South Carbrian

Silly, Silly Me

A ll I am is like a clown,

Q ueen is as weird as my name,

E merald like a Minecraft emerald as we protect to play,

E njoying games with my friends is like a bathtub of candy,

N ot as annoying as a messy room,

A lthough I act like a child.

J ones is as popular as laughter,

O n the spot is like a cherry on top,

N ew toys are like a silly girl eating ice cream,

E very good thing is like Heaven,

S o the end is silly like a funny face.

Aqeena Jones (9)

St Mary's Catholic Primary School, Newcastle-Under-Lyme

...m A Place

...re crackling and glowing through

k... ...ne cold out of my body.
I co...e from high winds blowing and blowing,
Keeping me fresh and cool.
I come from a sun making me sweat and huff,
Which I miss now.
I come from a brother who plays cricket and
is mean,
Which angers me sometimes.
I come from the smell of animals and dogs,
Which fills me with joy.
I come from kind loving friends keeping me happy,
Every day of my life.
I come from traditional activities,
Rushing through my veins all day.
I come from the presence of nature filling me
With joy and keeping me intrigued.
I come from the moon
Majestically shining through the night.
I come from the fiery wind of the sun

Keeping me happy forever.
I come from the barks and woofs
That fill my ears when heard.

Athulya Edirisingha (9)
St Mary's Catholic Primary School, South Moor

I Come From A Place

I come from my soft comforting teddy, Big Bear,
Who sleeps with me every night.
I come from the smell of horses,
And the sound of thundering hooves.
I come from the smell of mac 'n' cheese,
That melts on my tongue ever so slightly.
I come from the sight of ginger dog hair lying on
the ground,
And the crunch of kibble going down a treat.
I come from the sight of bright, green fields,
And the dream to have miles to roam free.
I come from the feel of a fleece duvet,
Keeping me warm during the cold nights.
I come from St Mary's Catholic Primary School,
Learning about loads of different things.
I come from the lovely sight of books,
The long pages of words and adventure.

Mia Purdy (10)
St Mary's Catholic Primary School, South Moor

I Come From A Place

I come from a place of cats,
I come from a place of water gun fights,
I come from a place of parks, adventures, and trees,
I come from a place of video games,
I come from a place of PlayStations, Xbox, and Nintendos,
I come from a place of lakes and forests,
I come from playing virtual reality,
I come from a place with birds, dogs, cats and pets,
I come from a place of curiosity,
I come from a place of ruins, castles, woods, and mysterious artwork,
I come from a love for Star Wars, movies, TV shows and genres.

Lewis Trelease (10)

St Mary's Catholic Primary School, South Moor

I Come From A Place

I come from the smell of perfume and herbs.
I come from theatre filling me with laughter
and happiness!
I come from my mam and dad making home-
cooked meals.
I come from crystals and gothic things.
I come from the haunted buildings!
I come from castles, ruins and museums.
I come from my cat and dog playing in the garden
and fighting sometimes.
I come from my garden.
I come from my dog barking and my cat meowing.
I come from theatre.
I come from piano.
I come from violin.
I come from nature.
I come from the forests.
I come from my garden.
I come from my annoying brother.
I come from my family.

I come from Earth!
I come from County Durham!

Rana Ozbek (10)
St Mary's Catholic Primary School, South Moor

I Come From A Place

I come from the smell of perfume.
I come from gymnastics filling me with joy.
I come from chicken nuggets.
I come from sports every week.
I come from people screaming.
I come from playing outside.
I come from dogs barking.
I come from cats running everywhere.
I come from dance.
I come from swimming.
I come from boxing.
I come from beautiful gardens.
I come from nature.
I come from forests, woods and scary animals.
I come from Sunday dinner.
I come from playing with friends.
I come from scrunchies.
I come from my mam.
I come from my dad.
I come from God.
I come from the Earth.

I come from Durham.
I come from Stanley.

Maddie Corby (9)
St Mary's Catholic Primary School, South Moor

I Come From A Place

I come from football,
I come from lots of football boots,
I come from football pitches.

I come from lots of cheering,
Goalkeeping gloves making my hands sweat,
Dogs barking in my ear.

I come from the smell of sweets and chocolate,
I come from a football but that is not all,
I come from blooming flowers.

I come from my loving family,
I come from my gran,
I come from home.

I come from Mr Boyle,
I come from Miss Neasham,
I come from class 5.

Gracie McArdle (9)
St Mary's Catholic Primary School, South Moor

I Come From A Place

I come from a tidy room with teddies at the back of my bed.

I come from football practice and games.

I come from video games with music to delight my ears and sing catchy songs.

I come from dogs barking and the smell of tea.

I come from rainy days and snow falling in the air.

I come from not being able to sleep and cuddling parents.

I come from chats with my brother and saving money.

I come from social media and running laps of my house.

William Leighton (9)

St Mary's Catholic Primary School, South Moor

I Come From A Place

I come from a silent, beautiful garden
Cashmere soap
The love of God.
I come from a warm bright house
A fire keeping me warm
I come from blankets wrapping me up.
I come from a stuttering voice
But that is not all I am
I can sing and dance.
I come from songs of my brother
Aids helping me hear
Pens and pencils doodling.
I come from dyslexia stuck in my brain
I get lost in my drawings
I come from everything.

Aerys Gray (10)
St Mary's Catholic Primary School, South Moor

I Come From A Place

I come from my garden,
It is all bright and sunny,
But it's small.

I come from a park,
Playing football,
With my friends.

I come from God's hands,
God's love,
And God's footsteps.

I come from my family,
And friends,
With care share and love.

I come from my school,
All the teachers,
And the headteacher.

I come from my parent helping me,
Teachers helping me,
And my family helping me.

Charleigh Gardner (10)
St Mary's Catholic Primary School, South Moor

I Come From A Place

I come from more than twenty pets,
I come from wooden swords and shields clashing,
I come from reading comics and horror,
I come from watching cute cartoons,
I come from watching and loving live action,
I come from eating popcorn and getting scared,
I come from playing golf,
I come from a place of balls being hit,
I come from PlayStations 2, 4 and 5,
I come from old SEGA consoles and original Sonic.

Dylan Gibson (10)

St Mary's Catholic Primary School, South Moor

I Come From A Place

I come from a sporting background,
I am a workout winger,
A football fanatic.

I come from fresh fruits,
Vegetation comes next,
Meat straight from the butchers.

I come from a lot of family,
Most tall but some short,
But we're all family.

I come from not much money,
Cheap food and clothes,
But I'm still grateful.

I come from a silent garden,
Glass windows glistening,
Trees swaying slowly.

Ryan Ingram (9)

St Mary's Catholic Primary School, South Moor

I Come From A Place

I come from a music background,
Listening to Shawn Mendes singing,
It is in my blood.

I come from a gaming background,
That's when I play FIFA 22,
And score 54 goals.

I come from a basketballing background,
Where I shoot five baskets in a row,
That's why they call me the champion.

I come from a footballing background,
Where I have my kit on,
Saving tremendous amounts of chances.

Mason Proctor (10)
St Mary's Catholic Primary School, South Moor

I Come From A Place

I come from my nana's house
A town called Stanley
Singing and listening to Ed Sheeran

I come from pets like dogs and lots more
Also my grandad's new dog, it keeps me warm
And I like hairy, fluffy, fuzzy dogs

I come from video games
Playing with my friends
Climbing with my friends

I come from a sport called football
Playing with my friends
Dribbling down the pitch while running.

Mackenzie Brunskill (10)
St Mary's Catholic Primary School, South Moor

I Come From A Place

I come from a silent garden,
Because I like the nature,
With the birds twittering in my head.

I come from exploring the nature,
Looking out for the clear sky,
So, I go into the wildness to explore.

I come from the sports,
In and outside to play sports,
Always having fun all the way.

I come from a lovely singing voice,
Singing when I hear a song,
Listening to the beats.

Mitchell Walton (10)
St Mary's Catholic Primary School, South Moor

I Come From A Place

I come from football
With my friends and family
I come from music

I come from the smell of candles
I come from the smell of potatoes
I come from the beach
I come from basketball

I come from games with my cousins
And my nanna and grandad
I come from South Moor in England.

Harry Stanger (10)
St Mary's Catholic Primary School, South Moor

I Come From A Place

I come from a gaming setup
I come from sunflowers
I come from a special sister
I come from a dyslexic brother
I come from a wonderful home
I come from a fabulous mam.

Charlie Marsden (9)
St Mary's Catholic Primary School, South Moor

Me

I am special and unique,
I am happy and emotional, always reaching for the stars.
Me, me, me!

I am special and unique,
Always searching for my dreams.
Me, me, me!

I am special and unique,
Can be light as a luscious pool staring at the shining sun.
Can have rage like a tiger stalking mysteriously in the fluffy snow.
Me, me, me!

Never can be guessed, with my mind full of unique balls shooting out of old, rusty cannons.

Me, starring, standing, calm as a tree, wet as a rainforest.
I am special and unique like everything!

Aris Roussias (8)
St Mary's CE Academy Walkley, Sheffield

That's Who I Am

My name is Ledjo
I am always nice and funny
I like to sing like G-Balvin.
My other talent is on the pitch
When the ball rolls into my feet
The destiny of the game has already switched.
My name is Ledjo and
I am an amazing superstar.
Let the history talk
And you hear it wherever you are.
All my family is proud of me that's why they love
me constantly.

Ledjon Mustafa (9)

St Mary's CE Academy Walkley, Sheffield

That's Who I Am

Hello, my name is Zeenat,
I am nine years old,
I live in a household
With a supportive family of my own.
In the future, I would like to become a doctor
To help people across the world
To change their sadness to happiness.
Never give up,
Always chase your dreams.

Zeenat Ahmadi
St Mary's CE Academy Walkley, Sheffield

That's Who I Am

I am individual, I am different, I am me!
I want to be a doctor, yes a doctor!
I am dyslexic, but that will not stop me!
I love to skate all the time, even when things are
not going well.
I love reading as it is always fun!
I am Jobey, I am different, I am individual.

Jobey Ramjiani (9)
St Mary's CE Academy Walkley, Sheffield

That's Who I Am

There are many sides to me
I am brave
Bold
Inquisitive
Confident
But shy when I don't know people.
Enough is what I am
Kind and shiny, caring and glowing
Crafty
Scientific
Terrific
That's what I am.

Tara Adesola (9)
St Mary's CE Academy Walkley, Sheffield

That's Who I Am

H i my name is Hazel
A nd I desperately want to go to the
Z oo to see animals like giraffes
E lephants and tigers, oh and I can't forget...
L ions.

Hazel McMahon (9)
St Mary's CE Academy Walkley, Sheffield

That's Who I Am

M iles Russell gets into hustles
I like bananas
L ook at me and I like to
E at junk food
S o I like eating food because I am Miles.

Miles Russell (9)
St Mary's CE Academy Walkley, Sheffield

This Is Me!

Dirt bikes are sweet and so are flowers,
Some I eat, some I devour.

Climb up high into the sky then fly down like a kite,
That's alright, I won't give up the fight.

Pizza is my favourite, especially when it's cheesy,
Washed down with a can of Sprite or Pepsi.

I love to learn about the planets,
I'd really like to spot a gannet.

That's the end of me,
I'm a boy,
This is me!

Harry England (10)
Walford Primary School, Walford

About Me

Football and rugby
My two favourite sports
Team sports
I play with my friends.

Taller than short
My favourite animal
Fur and four legs
He is a dog.

Computer games
I like to play
Fortnite is my favourite
I play with my friends.

Mario Bundy (11)
Walford Primary School, Walford

This Is Me!

I stand tall and proud
But mostly tall
As rainbows fill the ground
As crystals shimmer in the moon
I sit on the ground
I read or I draw the world away
As my cat lies there
Only wanting tummy rubs from me.

Arrianne Marangon (11)
Walford Primary School, Walford

This Is Me!

I am helpful,
I am meaningful,
I help others a lot,
No matter what other people think,
I will be there by your side,
You can tell me anything,
I am your friend and I do care,
This is me!

Maisie Walton (11)
Walford Primary School, Walford

This Is Me

Buddy and me,
Playing football all day long,
Running around.

Buddy and me,
Watching TV,
Playing in the garden.

Buddy and me,
Going for walks,
Playing tug of war.

Tyler Spiers (9)
Walford Primary School, Walford

What Makes Me? This Is Me!

Two cups of kindness,
A field to play cricket,
A tub of flexibility,
Three tablespoons of helpfulness,
Two tubs of gymnastics,
A tablespoon of bendiness,
A football,
This is me!

Isla Matthews (11)

Walford Primary School, Walford

This Is Me!

I am a super striker,
I am a super footballer,
I am a football champion.

I like playing 'Around the World',
I like doing rainbow flicks,
I like playing with my team.

Zach Davies (9)
Walford Primary School, Walford

This Is Me!

I dream of finding what I am good at,
I want to be a book writer,
Hair as blonde as the sun,
Eyes as brown as the night-time,
Animal lover,
I have a dog and a hamster.

Clemie Goodison
Walford Primary School, Walford

This Is Me

I am a basketball striker,
I am a dog lover,
I am a Star Wars fan.

I love Baby Yoda,
I love writing,
I love Harry Potter,
I love pizza,
I love Xbox.

Max Bain (9)

Walford Primary School, Walford

Sophie

S chool is fun, spaghetti is delicious

O range is my favourite colour and Oliver is my friend

P laying on the iPad and playing in the park

H appy, honest and helpful are things that I am

I estyn is another friend I have and I love Ice cream

E ach of these things makes me... Sophie!

Sophie McGuiness (11)

Ysgol Hen Felin, Ystrad

Amazing Family

My mammy is amazing
She drives a black car
She has black hair
She is nice
I love her

Priya is a baby girl
She is my sister
She is cute
She has black hair too
I love her

Max is my puppy dog
He is dark brown and light brown
He is a good boy
He likes to play in the house
I love him

My name is Alicia
I love Mammy, Priya and Max.

Alicia Jones (10)

Ysgol Hen Felin, Ystrad

Red

Roses are red
And they smell nice

Strawberries are red
And they are yummy

My jumper is red
And it is comfy

Red is my favourite colour.

Phoebe Lloyd Szigetvari (11)

Ysgol Hen Felin, Ystrad

My Trip To The Park

Playing in the park
Shooting down the slide
Green grass all around
Swinging on the swings
Sun is shining
I am eating ice cream.

Jason Jones
Ysgol Hen Felin, Ystrad

YoungWriters® Est. 1991

YOUNG WRITERS INFORMATION

We hope you have enjoyed reading this book – and that you will continue to in the coming years.

If you're the parent or family member of an enthusiastic poet or story writer, do visit our website **www.youngwriters.co.uk/subscribe** and sign up to receive news, competitions, writing challenges and tips, activities and much, much more! There's lots to keep budding writers motivated!

If you would like to order further copies of this book, or any of our other titles, then please give us a call or order via your online account.

Young Writers
Remus House
Coltsfoot Drive
Peterborough
PE2 9BF
(01733) 890066
info@youngwriters.co.uk

Join in the conversation!
Tips, news, giveaways and much more!

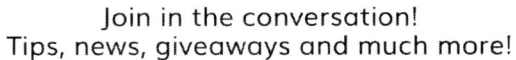

 **YoungWritersUK**    **YoungWritersCW**    **youngwriterscw**